THE OMELETTE COOKBOOK

Table of Contents:

1. Omelette With Goat Cheese and Asparagus

Prep Time: 10 minutes
Cook Time: 12 minutes
Ready In: In less than 1 hour
Servings: 2 - 3

INGREDIENTS:

3 pieces large eggs
1 tablespoon butter
1 tablespoon olive oil
2 tablespoons goat cheese (crumbled)
salt and pepper to taste

DIRECTIONS:

1. Preheat oven (350 degrees F). Cut the dry ends of the asparagus after rinsing it with water. Drizzle the baking sheet with olive oil and then place the dry ends on it. Sprinkle with freshly ground pepper and salt then bake for about 8 to 10 minutes. When done, remove from the oven. Make sure to cut into pieces (1 inch).

2. In a large bowl, crack the eggs and season with salt and pepper. Use a wire whisk in mixing it well.

3. Use a non-stick frying pan and a medium heat low. Put the butter until it melts and forms bubbles. Then add the egg mixture. You may use a fork to stir the mixture before placing it on the pan. Allow the egg to cook, gently lifting its sides until the egg is uniformly cooked. Add the asparagus and goat cheese. Using a spatula, gently fold the omelet over onto itself. Then, serve immediately.

2. **Omelette with Masala**

Prep Time: 5 minutes
Cook Time: 5 minutes
Ready In: Less than 1 hour
Servings: 2 - 3

INGREDIENTS:

4 eggs
2 tablespoons oil or butter
2 tablespoons Coriander leaves (finely chopped)
1/4 teaspoon Garam masala powder
1/4 teaspoon Turmeric powder
1/4 teaspoon Black pepper powder
4 tablespoons carrot (finely minced)
4 tablespoons capsicum (finely minced)
2 tablespoons milk
2 green chilies (finely minced)
4 shallots (finely chopped); 4 tablespoons of small onions will do
salt

DIRECTIONS:

1. In a bowl, beat the eggs until frothy. With a wire whisk, add all the ingredients, except oil.

2. Drizzle a non-stick pan with oil and heat to medium low. Once hot, put the egg mixture until the sides are cooked. Gently slip over in order to cook the other side of the omelette.

3. Serve immediately. You can sprinkle it with grated cheese, shredded chicken, mushroom, or other vegetables.

3. Omelette with Spinach and Feta Cheese

Prep Time: 15 minutes
Cook Time: 10 minutes
Ready In: Less than 1 hour
Servings: 4

INGREDIENTS:

1 tablespoon olive oil
1 pack (10 ounce) chopped frozen spinach; thawed and squeezed dry
8 large eggs
1/2 cup feta cheese (crumbled)
1/2 teaspoon salt (divided)
1 teaspoon dried oregano (divided)
1 cup halved grape tomatoes
black pepper to taste

DIRECTIONS:

1. Heat a non-stick pan to a medium low. Meanwhile, mix 1/2 tsp. salt, 1/2 oregano, and pepper in a small bowl. Add feta cheese.

2. In a medium bowl, beat the eggs using a wire whisk. Then, add spinach, 1/4 tsp. salt, and 1/2 tsp oregano. Put salt and pepper to taste. Drizzle the pan with oil. Increase the heat to medium high. Place the egg mixture, making sure the mixture is evenly spread on the pan. Cook for 3 minutes until the egg is cooked yet moist. Reduce the heat and then pour the tomato mixture over the half portion of the omelet. Carefully fold the untopped half portion over the filling with the use of a spatula. After a minute or two, place it on a plate. Cut into pieces and serve immediately.

4. **Omelette Cups with Quinoa**

Prep Time: 10 minutes
Cook Time: 40 minutes
Ready In: Less than 1 hour
Servings: 12 regular cups

INGREDIENTS:

2 eggs
1/4 teaspoon garlic salt
1 tablespoon Frank's red hot sauce
1/2 cup Daiya Vegan cheese
2 cups diced veggies (avocado, cauliflower, mixed bell peppers, onion)
1 cup egg whites
2 cups Quinoa (cooked and cooled)
salt and pepper

DIRECTIONS:

1. Preheat oven (350 degrees F). In a bowl, whisk eggs and egg whites together until blended. Add all other ingredients such as cheese and Quinoa, spices, and veggies.

2. Spray your muffin tin with a non-stick cooking spray. Scoop even amount of the Quinoa omelette mixture into the muffin tins. Put inside the oven and then bake for about 40 minutes.

3. Remove the muffin tins from the oven and let it cool. And then remove the omelette cups. Serve immediately.

5. **Omelette with Potatoes and Chives**

Prep Time: 10 minutes
Cook Time: 25 minutes
Ready In: Less than 1 hour
Servings: 2

INGREDIENTS:

5 large eggs
1 tablespoon chopped chives
1 tablespoon butter (unsalted)
3 tablespoons milk
1 cup Yukon Gold potatoes (unpeeled; diced)
3 slices thick-cut bacon (must be cut into pieces)
1 tablespoon olive oil
Kosher salt
freshly ground pepper

DIRECTIONS:

1. Preheat oven (350 degrees F).

2. Use an ovenproof omelet pan. Place the pan over medium heat. Drizzle it with olive oil and cook bacon for about 3 minutes. Make sure the bacon is browned yet not crispy. Place the bacon in a small bowl and set aside.

3. Take a pan and place the potatoes. Cook, sprinkle with pepper and salt. Continue cooking for about 10 minutes. Remove from heat and put the potatoes together with the bacon.

4. Meanwhile, beat the eggs and then stir in milk in a medium bowl. Put 1/2 teaspoon salt, then add 1/4 teaspoon pepper. Using the same pan, discard the oil and then put butter. Put the heat to low and pour the egg mixture. Put the potatoes, bacon, and chives on top, making sure everything is sprinkled evenly. Place the pan inside the oven and bake for 8 minutes. Remove from the oven, divide in half, and then serve immediately.

6. Omelette with Gruyere and Sausage

Prep Time: 10 minutes
Cook Time: 33 minutes
Ready In: Less than 1 hour
Servings: 4 - 6

INGREDIENTS:

8 large eggs
butter
1/2 pound turkey sausage (casings must be removed)
1 small onion (diced)
2 tablespoons olive oil
1/4 cup and 2 tablespoons fresh flat-leaf parsley (chopped)
1 1/2 cups Gruyere cheese (grated)
1 red bell pepper (diced)
freshly ground black pepper
kosher salt
1/3 cup whole milk

DIRECTIONS:

1. Preheat oven (425 degrees F). Take an 8 x 8 baking dish and lightly spread the butter.

2. Heat a skillet over medium-high heat and then cook onion for 3 minutes. Add the sausage and mix until cooked. Set aside the pan.

3. In a bowl, beat the eggs together with milk. Sprinkle salt and pepper. Add the red bell pepper, followed 1 cup Gruyere cheese and only 1/4 cup parsley. Add in the onion-sausage mixture. After which, pour the batter into the baking dish. Sprinkle with cheese and bake for about 25 minutes.

4. Remove from the oven and then cut the omelet into wedges. Use the remaining parsley and sprinkle it over the omelet. Serve and enjoy!

7. Omelette with Chili

Prep Time: 10 minutes
Cook Time: 10 minutes
Ready In: Less than 1 hour
Servings: 1 - 2

INGREDIENTS:

sour cream (for garnish)
2 large eggs
1/4 cup chives (chopped)
2 tablespoons butter (unsalted)
1 package (8 ounce) 3-cheese Mexican cheese (shredded)
1 can vegetarian chili with beans
1/2 pound breakfast sausage links

DIRECTIONS:

1. Cut the sausage into chunks, about 1/4 inch. Using a medium pan, cook the sausage over medium-low heat. Add the chili and cook for about 5 minutes.

2. Meanwhile, use another skillet and melt the butter over medium-low heat. Beat the eggs and sprinkle 1/8 cup chives. Pour the mixture into the pan and cook. Put the sausage and chili mixture on the half portion of the omelet, reserve the 1/4 cup. After which, put a layer of cheese, reserve 1/4 cup.

3. Gently fold the omelet. Use the remaining chili and cheese and put them on top. Place the omelet on a place and sprinkle with the remaining chives. Garnish it with sour cream.

8. Omelette with Cilantro and Serrano Chile

Prep Time: 15 minutes
Cook Time: 5 minutes
Ready In: Less than 1 hour
Servings: 4

INGREDIENTS:

6 eggs
2 tablespoons canola oil
3/4 teaspoon turmeric
3/4 teaspoon paprika
2 tablespoons fresh cilantro leaves (minced)
1 serrano chile (minced; remove the seeds if you do not like too much spice)
3/4 cup red onion (finely minced)
kosher salt and black pepper to taste

DIRECTIONS:

1. Using a wire whisk, beat the eggs and add in onion, turmeric, paprika, cilantro, and chili. Blend well. Sprinkle a pinch of salt and pepper.

2. Drizzle a non-stick skillet with oil. Heat over medium-high heat. Pour the mixture into the skillet, making sure that the chile, cilantro, and onions are evenly distributed around the pan. Cover the pan and cook for about 3 minutes. Uncover the pan and gently flip the omelet over to cook the other side. Take another minute to cook it but do not cover anymore.

3. Cut into 4 slices and serve.

9. **Omelette with Smoked Salmon**

Prep Time: 5 minutes
Cook Time: 5 minutes
Ready In: Less than 1 hour
Servings: 2

INGREDIENTS:

2 eggs
1 tablespoon black lumpfish caviar
2 tablespoons smoked salmon (chopped)
1/4 cup softened chives and onion light cream cheese
1/2 teaspoon dried dill
1/2 teaspoon Dijon mustard
3 tablespoons sour cream
chives (minced); optional

DIRECTIONS:

1. In a small bowl, mix the following ingredients together: mustard, dill, and sour cream. Set aside. In another small bowl, mix chopped smoked salmon and cream cheese together. Set aside.

2. Take a non-stick frying pan and sprinkle it with a cooking spray. Use medium heat. Beat the eggs and pour into the pan. Cook for about 3 minutes. Take the salmon mixture and scoop half of it on the half side of the omelet, folding in half. Use the remaining mixture for another set of omelet.

3. Pour the dill mixture onto the omelet. Garnish it with chives and caviar.

10. Omelette Cup with Ham & Peppers

Prep Time: 5 minutes
Cook Time: 5 minutes
Ready In: Less than 1 hour
Servings: 1

INGREDIENTS:

Serving suggestion - Whole Wheat English muffin
orange slices (optional)
2 tablespoons fat-free cheddar cheese (shredded)
1 ounce fat-free ham (chopped)
1/2 cup liquid egg substitute (fat-free)
2 tablespoons onion (chopped)
1/4 cup green bell pepper (chopped)

DIRECTIONS:

1. Get a microwave-safe mug and spray it with a non-stick spray. Combine pepper and onion together and then microwave for about 2 minutes, until softened.

2. After which, add egg substitute. Put inside the microwave for about 1 minute. Add ham and cheese. Stir gently. Microwave for about 1 minute.

3. Remove from the microwave and garnish with orange slices. Serve immediately with English muffins.

11. Omelette with Strawberries and Whip Cream

Prep Time: 10 minutes
Cook Time: 15 minutes
Ready In: Less than 1 hour
Servings: 2 - 3

Strawberries:

8 pcs. medium strawberries (thinly sliced)
1 tablespoon white wine vinegar
2 tablespoons sugar (granulated)

Omelet:

4 eggs
1/2 tablespoon extra virgin olive oil
1 tablespoon butter (unsalted, at room temperature)
1 tablespoons fresh mint (finely chopped)
kosher salt
1 tablespoon heavy cream
2 tablespoons granulated sugar

Whipped Cream:

1 teaspoon vanilla extract
1 1/2 teaspoons powdered sugar
1/2 cup heavy whipping cream

DIRECTIONS:

1. In a small bowl, combine strawberries, vinegar, and granulated sugar together. Set aside for 15 minutes and then strain before using.

2. In making the omelet, beat the eggs together with cream, granulated sugar, and salt. Add the mint. Meanwhile, combine oil and butter in a non-stick pan and heat over medium-high heat. Pour the egg mixture, then cook for 4 minutes. Pour the strawberry mixture on the center of the omelet. Fold the edges. Cook for 3 minutes.

3. Meanwhile, combine vanilla, powdered sugar, and cream together until you create a whipped cream. Cut the omelet and garnish with whipped cream.

12. Omelette with Steak and Spinach

Prep Time: 15 minutes
Cook Time: 10 minutes
Ready In: Less than 1 hour
Servings: 2

Leftovers:
5 eggs
1 tablespoon butter (unsalted)
1/8 teaspoon ground pepper
1/8 teaspoon salt
2 tablespoons club soda
3 ounces cheddar (shredded)
2 ounces fresh spinach (cooked)
3 ounces thinly sliced steak (cooked)
1/8 baking powder

1. Preheat the broiler. In a pan, saute steak and spinach. Add in all ingredients except butter. In a blender, process cheese and leftovers for about 10 seconds. Add baking powder and club soda.

2. In a huge non-stick pan, melt the butter. Pour the egg mixture. With the use of a rubber spatula, gently push the cooked egg from the side of the bottom of the pan to the other side in order to create height. This will allow the new raw egg to reach the pan's bottom.

3. Flip the omelet to cook the other side. Remove the omelet from heat and fill its center with the cheese and leftover feeling. Then, fold it in half. Slice into pieces and serve.

13. **Omelette with Ricotta and Zucchini**

Prep Time: 25 minutes
Cook Time: 15 minutes
Ready In: Less than 1 hour
Servings: 4

INGREDIENTS:

12 eggs (slightly beaten)
1 cup baby arugula leaves
small wedge Parmigiano-Reggiano
1 small bunch scallions; greens and whites (chopped)
1 roasted sweet red pepper (chopped)
1 red chile pepper (thinly sliced or chopped)
1 pound small firm zucchini (finely chopped)
3 tablespoons extra virgin olive oil
2 tablespoons thyme leaves (finely chopped)
1/3 to 1/2 cup whole milk
1 cup fresh ricotta
salt and pepper to taste

DIRECTIONS:

1. In a bowl, mix ricotta with thyme, pepper, and salt. Get a cake pan and line it with plastic wrap. Take a non-stick skillet which is similar to the size of your cake pan.

2. Whisk the eggs and season with salt and pepper. Get two plates which are similar to the size of your skillet. In the skillet, heat the extra virgin olive oil over medium-high heat. Add 1/3 zucchini, sweet peppers, chili, and scallions. Sprinkle with salt and pepper. Saute the ingredients together and pour in 1/3 of the eggs. Cook until browned. Get the plate and cover the pan. Flip the omelet to cook the other side. Repeat the same process to create 3 omelets.

3. On a plate, place one omelet and then spread the ricotta mixture over the top. Place the other omelet over the top of the first omelet. Sprinkle with cheese. And then put the third omelet. Garnish with Parmesan cheese and serve.

14. Omelette with Crabmeat

Prep Time: 15 minutes
Cook Time: 15 minutes
Ready In: Less than 1 hour
Servings: 4

INGREDIENTS:

16 eggs
1 1/2 cups lump crabmeat
4 tablespoons butter (unsalted)
1 large onion (chopped)
black pepper and salt to taste
2 tablespoons mayonnaise
1 1/2 cups celery (chopped)
1/4 cup fresh parsley leaves (chopped)
1 teaspoon crab boil seasoning

DIRECTIONS:

1. Get a large bowl and combine the following: mayonnaise, crab boil seasoning, crabmeat, parsley, onion, pepper and salt, and celery. The mayonnaise will moisten the mixture.

2. Use a non-stick pan and melt 1 tablespoon butter. Use medium heat. Pour in 1/4 of the crab mixture for about 10 minutes or until the onions and celery are crisp yet tender. Meanwhile, get a large bowl and whisk the eggs. Pour in 1/4 of the whipped eggs into the crab mixture.

3. Cook the omelet. Use a spatula to gently pull the edges toward its center. Flip the omelet to cook the other side. Once done, serve immediately.

15. Omelette with Beef Stew

Prep Time: 5 minutes
Cook Time: 7 minutes
Ready In: Less than 1 hour
Servings: 4

INGREDIENTS:

1 cup beef stew
4 teaspoons butter
salt and pepper
3 tablespoons parsley (finely chopped)
2 tablespoons sesame oil
1 1/2 tablespoons soy sauce
3 eggs; 8 eggs
1/2 cup Portuguese sausage (diced)
1/2 cup shrimp (diced)
1/2 cup roasted pork (shredded)
1/2 cup green onions (chopped)
3 cups cooked white rice
1/4 cup peanut oil

DIRECTIONS:

1. Heat the peanut oil in a wok. Then add the cooked rice. Toss until golden brown. Add in the shrimp, sausage, pork, and green onions. Toss in the garlic, soy sauce, 3 eggs, parsley, and sesame oil. Stir fry for about 2 minutes. Sprinkle salt and pepper.

2. Meanwhile, beat the 8 eggs together in a large mixing bowl. Sprinkle salt and pepper to taste. In a non-stick pan, melt the butter over medium-high heat. Pour in 1/4 of the egg mixture into the pan. Use a fork to scramble the eggs. Let it cook for about 1 minute. Flip it over to cook the other side. Spoon an ample amount of the beef stew down the center of the omelet. Then, put the fried rice in a large, shallow bowl. Gently slide the omelet onto the rice, flipping its half over the other. Garnish with parsley.

16. Omelette with Swiss and American cheeses

Prep Time: 10 minutes
Cook Time: 5 minutes
Ready In: Less than 1 hour
Servings: 1 large omelet

INGREDIENTS:

3 eggs
1 cup chili (cooked)
1 slice American cheese
1 slice Swiss cheese
1/2 cup bacon (cooked, diced)
1/2 cup ham (diced)
1/2 cup onion (diced)
1/2 cup potato (tender, diced)

DIRECTIONS:

1. In a blender, put the eggs and mix until it's almost white.

2. On a grill pan, put the onion, ham, potato, and bacon. Saute for about 30 seconds. Add in the egg mixture over it. Cook the omelet until its edges are slightly firm.

3. Add the slices of cheese. Flip its half over the other. Cook for another 2 minutes. Place it on a plate and serve with bean chili or cooked meat.

17. **Omelette with Potatoes and Garlic**

Prep Time: 15 minutes
Cook Time: 25 minutes
Ready In: Less than 1 hour
Servings: 4

INGREDIENTS:

8 large eggs
1/2 tablespoon fresh lime juice
2 tablespoons cilantro (chopped)
1/2 cup pepper jack cheese (shredded)
1 1/4 cups plum tomatoes (coarsely chopped)
coarse salt and freshly ground pepper
2 scallions (thinly sliced)
2 cloves garlic (finely chopped)
1 red-skinned potato (well scrubbed and thinly sliced)
2 tablespoons olive oil

DIRECTIONS:

1. In a broiler-proof skillet, heat the oil over medium-low heat. Cook potato for about 10 minutes or until golden brown. Add in all other ingredients except for the scallions. Sprinkle with salt and pepper. Cook for about 1 minute.

2. Beat eggs well in a large bowl. Add 1/4 cup of cheese and tomato. Blend well. Pour in the remaining oil to the pan. Then pour the egg mixture over potatoes.

3. Preheat the broiler, with rack which must be 4 inches away from the heat. Meanwhile, on the stovetop, cook the eggs. Lift the edges gently to allow all the mixture to cook. Sprinkle the remaining cheese on top of the omelet. After which, broil in the oven for about 2 minutes.

4. To make a salsa, mix the remaining tomatoes, cilantro, lime juice, and scallions together. Use a metal spatula to remove the omelet from the pan. Slide it onto a platter. Cut into wedges and serve with salsa.

18. Omelette with Calvados

Prep Time: 10 minutes
Cook Time: 15 minutes
Ready In: Less than 1 hour
Servings: 4

INGREDIENTS:

4 large eggs
4 tablespoons Calvados (apple-flavored brandy can be an alternative)
kosher salt
1/2 teaspoon vanilla extract
powdered sugar
1 tablespoon and 1 teaspoon sugar
1 tablespoon and 1 teaspoon all-purpose flour
1/3 cup heavy cream
2 tablespoons butter (unsalted, divided); 4 teaspoons butter at room temperature (unsalted)

DIRECTIONS:

1. In a medium bowl, blend cream, eggs, vanilla, sugar, flour, and salt together using a wire whisk.

2. In a non-stick skillet, melt 1/2 tablespoon butter over medium-high heat. Pour 1/3 cup of the batter and cook for about 2 minutes or until golden brown. To cook the other side, flip the omelet. Add 1 tablespoon Calvados. Return it to heat until Calvados thickens a bit.

3. Place the omelet on a plate and then fold into thirds. While hot, spread a teaspoon of butter over it and then dust some powdered sugar on top. Use the remaining mixture to make 4 omelets, all in all.

19. Omelette with Olives and Fennel

Prep Time: 10 minutes
Cook Time: 15 minutes
Ready In: 1 hour 15 minutes
Servings: 8

INGREDIENTS:

8 cherry tomatoes
5 large eggs (beaten and sprinkled with salt and pepper)
1 1/2 tablespoons fresh dill (chopped)
2 tablespoons olive oil (divided)
1/2 4-ounce package crumbled goat cheese (seasoned with sweet red pepper, basil, and thyme)
1/4 cup pitted green brine-cured olives (chopped)
2 cups fresh fennel bulb (thinly sliced and chopped)

DIRECTIONS:

1. In a non-stick skillet, heat the oil (only 1 tablespoon) over medium-high heat. Saute fennel bulb for about 5 minutes. When cooked and softened, add tomatoes. Use fork to mash them. Add in olives. Sprinkle salt and pepper. Pour the mixture to a bowl.

2. Using the same skillet, drizzle it with the remaining oil and heat over medium-high heat. Beat the eggs and pour the mixture and cook for about 3 minutes. Drizzle half of the omelet with half of the cheese and then sprinkle the fennel mixture. Then top with dill and then sprinkle the remaining cheese. Fold the other half of the omelet over the filling using a spatula. Slide onto a plate and garnish with some chopped fennel fronds.

20. Omelette with Hashbrowns and Salsa

Prep Time: 10 minutes
Cook Time: 10 minutes
Ready In: Less than 1 hour
Servings: 1 - 2

INGREDIENTS:

2 large eggs
A variety of ingredients (cheese, salsa, hash browns)
salt and pepper to taste

DIRECTIONS:

1. Get a quart-size Ziploc freezer bag. Crack the eggs and pour into the bag. Shake the bag to combine the eggs well.

2. Put the ingredients of your choice. You may put cheese, green and red bell peppers, tomatoes, ham, and other ingredients you want to include. Sprinkle pepper and salt to taste.

3. In a medium pot, boil 4 to 6 cups of water. When the water is already boiling, place the Ziploc bag into it, for about 13 minutes. When the omelet is already cooked, open the bag and slide the omelet onto the plate.

21. **Omelette with Spaghetti**

Prep Time: 10 minutes
Cook Time: 20 minutes
Ready In: Less than 1 hour
Servings: 2

INGREDIENTS:

4 eggs
4 sprigs parsley (minced)
5 to 6 basil leaves
5 tablespoons extra virgin olive oil
1 clove garlic (peeled and crushed)
1/2 pound mozzarella
2/3 pound spaghetti (300 grams)
2/3 pound chopped tomatoes (300 grams)
1/2 cup freshly grated parmigiano plus pecorino romano cheese
100 grams spicy italian sausage
salt and pepper

DIRECTION:

1. Bring pasta to boil. Meanwhile, heat 3 tablespoons olive oil over medium-high heat. Saute garlic and add tomatoes. Sprinkle with salt and pepper. Let it simmer for about 10 minutes. Then, add in the basil.

2. Slice the mozzarella cheese. Remove the casing of the sausage and slice it into pieces. When the water is already boiling, sprinkle some salt and cook the spaghetti.

3. In a large bowl, beat the eggs and season with parsley. Add half of the cheese mixture. Sprinkle with salt and pepper.

4. Drain the pasta. To cool it, run it under cold water. After which, pour the egg mixture. Meanwhile, in a large skillet, heat the remaining olive oil. Pour half of the pasta mixture and sprinkle with cheese, sausage, and tomatoes.

5. Use the remaining pasta to cover the tomato mixture. Cover the skillet and cook for about 5 minutes. See to it that a crust has formed at the bottom part of the frittata. Flip the skillet to cook the unbrowned side of the omelet. Place onto a plate and serve immediately.

22. Omelette with Oysters

Prep Time: 10 minutes
Cook Time: 15 minutes
Ready In: Less than 1 hour
Servings: 4

INGREDIENTS:

6 eggs (slightly beaten)
2 tablespoons corn flour
6 oysters (washed and cut into pieces)
4 stems spring onions (chopped)
2 teaspoons pepper
2 stems coriander (chopped)
4 tablespoons peanut oil
1 teaspoon sesame oil
salt and pepper to taste

DIRECTIONS:

1. In a small bowl, drizzle the pieces of oyster with corn flour. Set aside.

2. Beat the eggs and then add the chopped coriander and onions. Blanch the oyster in boiling water and then drain. Sprinkle some salt and pepper to taste. Add sesame oil. Blend well.

3. In a non-stick pan, heat the peanut oil. Pour half of both egg mixture and oyster mixture onto the pan. Cook until the omelet turn golden brown. Repeat the same process with the remaining egg and oyster mixtures.

4. Serve and enjoy!

23. Omelette with Coconut

Prep Time: 5 minutes
Cook Time: 10 minutes
Ready In: Less than 1 hour
Servings: 1

INGREDIENTS:

knob of butter
2 eggs
1/2 cup desiccated coconut
2 tablespoons sugar

DIRECTIONS:

1. In a small bowl, beat the eggs with wire whisk. Add the sugar and continue beating. Pour the coconut afterwards.

2. In a small non-stick frying pan, melt the butter. Pour in the egg mixture. Flip it over to cook the other side.

3. Place onto a plate and sprinkle with the remaining sugar. Can be served with a scoop of ice cream.

24. Omelette with Almonds and Maple Syrup

Prep Time: 5 minutes
Cook Time: 15 minutes
Ready In: Less than 1 hour
Servings: 2

INGREDIENTS:

1/2 teaspoon vanilla extract
3 eggs (separated)
1/4 cup slivered almonds
5 tablespoons pure maple syrup
salt

DIRECTIONS:

1. Preheat the oven (350 degrees F).

2. In a small bowl, beat the yolks and then add vanilla, syrup, and salt.

3. Meanwhile, in another small bowl, whip the egg whites until stiff peaks form. After which, fold the egg whites into the yolk mixture.

4. Get an oven safe pan and sprinkle some cooking spray. Add the almonds and then followed by the egg mixture. Cook over low heat for about 8 minutes. Then, transfer the pan to the oven and bake for about 8 minutes.

5. Serve immediately while hot.

25. Omelette with Corn Tortillas and Crawdad Tails

Prep Time: 10 minutes
Cook Time: 15 minutes
Ready In: Less than 1 hour
Servings: 1

INGREDIENTS:

3 large eggs
2 corn tortillas (soft fried or steamed)
a pat of butter
a bit of parsley or cilantro
1 small tomato (sliced into cubes)
1 dash of salsa Picante (optional)
1 tablespoon Nopalitos (chopped)
basel
2 portabella mushrooms
1/4 cup cheddar cheese
2 tablespoons beer (water can be a substitute)
1 piece avocado (ripe)
1/2 teaspoon cumin
10 crawdad tails (shrimp can also be used)

DIRECTIONS:

1. Cut the avocado, remove the seed, and slice into strips. Meanwhile, shell the crawdad tails. Afterwards, saute lightly and add salsa Picante. Set aside.

2. Cut the mushrooms into pieces. Grate the cheese. In a bowl, beat the eggs and then add in basil, FG pepper, cumin, and beer. Use a wire whisk to blend ingredients well.

3. Using an omelette pan, melt the butter and add in the egg mixture. Cook for about 1 minute and then lay in the crawdad tails. Put the mushrooms and then sprinkle with cheese and chopped Nopalitos. Then, fold the omelet when cooked. Meanwhile, lightly fry or steam the tortillas. Drizzle the omelet with tomato cubes and garnish with avocado slices. Serve immediately and enjoy.

26. Omelette with Corned Beef

Prep Time: 10 minutes
Cook Time: 15 minutes
Ready In: Less than 1 hour
Servings: 3 - 4

INGREDIENTS:

4 eggs
3 cups rice
salt and pepper to taste
2 tablespoons butter
1/2 cup pineapple tidbits
1/2 cup button mushrooms (chopped)
2 medium potatoes (diced)
dried basil leaves (chopped)
chinese 5 spices
3 tablespoons banana catsup
2 tablespoons hoisin sauce
1 teaspoon oyster sauce
1 thumb size ginger (finely chopped)
1 red onion (finely chopped)
210 gm corned beef
3 cloves garlic (finely chopped)

DIRECTIONS:

1.Using a frying pan, melt butter and saute garlic, onion, ginger, and potato. Pour the corned beef and saute. Drizzle some black pepper and add soy sauce, fivespices, oyster sauce, rice, mushroom, and hoisin sauce. Continue sauteing.

2.Pour in the pineapples and stir. Remove the pan from heat. Drizzle ample amount of catsup then sprinkle with salt and pepper. Blend well.

3. Meanwhile, in a bowl, beat the eggs. Sprinkle some pepper and salt. Add dried basils.

4. Fry the egg mixture on a non-stick pan. Place the omelet onto a plate and fill it with corned beef rice. Garnish and fold with catsup, dried basil leaves, and hoisin sauce.

27. **Omelette with Hashbrowns and Bacon**

Prep Time: 10 minutes
Cook Time: 10 minutes
Ready In: Less than 1 hour
Servings: 2

INGREDIENTS:

1/2 cup sour cream
1/2 cup cheddar cheese (grated)
frozen hash brown potatoes (for 2 servings)
6 tablespoons bacon (chopped)
green onions (diced)
salt and pepper to taste

DIRECTIONS:

1. Using a large non-stick skillet, fry hash browns with oil. One particular portion of the pan must be thicker in hash browns compared to the other.

2. As soon as the thinner side is cooked, spread cheese and drizzle some bacon. Put some sour cream on the thicker side, like an omelet. After which, fold in half.

3. Cover the pan and reduce the heat to medium-low. When the cheese has melted, remove the pan from heat.

4. Place onto a plate and garnish with bacon and green onions. Cut in half and serve immediately.

28.Omelette with Seaweed

Prep Time: 10 minutes
Cook Time: 20 minutes
Ready In: Less than 1 hour
Servings: 2

INGREDIENTS:

5 eggs
1/2 teaspoon garlic powder
1/2 small onions (finely chopped)
1/2 small carrot (finely chopped)
1 slice American or mozzarella cheese
1 tablespoon olive oil
1 sheet Korean roasted seaweed (optional)
salt and pepper to taste
1 green onion (finely chopped)

DIRECTIONS:

1. In a medium bowl, beat the eggs and add chopped onions, carrots, and green onions. Sprinkle some pepper and salt. Drizzle with a dash of garlic powder.

2. Pour the egg mixture in a non-stick skillet or pan. Use medium heat and cook for few minutes. When almost done, drizzle some cheese on top of the omelet.

3. With the use of a spatula or spoon, lift one side of the omelet and roll into a tight roll. Place it on a cutting board. Set aside to cool.

4. Slice the omelet into two and slide onto a plate. Serve and enjoy!

29. **Omelette with Kebab**

Prep Time: 15 minutes
Cook Time: 0 minutes
Ready In: 1 hour 15 minutes
Servings: 4

INGREDIENTS:

2 eggs
shredded cheese (optional)
2 tablespoons butter
2 tablespoon whole milk
Kebab ingredients (meat and vegetables; cut into pieces)
salt and pepper

DIRECTIONS:

1. In a small bowl, beat the eggs very well. Set aside.

2. Get a small non-stick pan and put the leftover Kebab over medium heat and then turn to low heat.

3. Heat another small non-stick frying pan and melt butter. Pour in the egg mixture, making sure that every part is cooked. Sprinkle some salt and pepper. Drizzle some cheese on the half portion of the omelet. Place the leftover Kebab over the cheese. Gently fold the omelet, using the unfilled portion to cover the part with fillings. Cook for about 1 minute.

4. Remove from pan and place onto a plate. Drizzle with cheese and serve immediately.

30. Omelette with Dark Chocolate

Prep Time: 15 minutes
Cook Time: 25 minutes
Ready In: Less than 1 hour
Servings: 8

INGREDIENTS:

20 grams butter (unsalted)
icing sugar (sifted)
1 tablespoon plain flour
2 tablespoons cream
1/4 cup caster sugar (55 grams)
6 eggs (separated)
120 grams raspberries
ice cream (optional)
120 grams dark chocolate (melted)

DIRECTIONS:

1. Preheat oven (190 degrees Celsius). Meanwhile, in a large bowl, beat the egg yolks together with cream, melted chocolate, flour, and sugar.

2. Beat the egg whites with an electric mixer until soft peaks are formed. After which, carefully fold the eggwhites into the chocolate mixture using a spatula.

3. In a large oven-proof frying pan, melt the butter over low heat. Add in half of the egg mixture. Bake for about 5 minutes, until puffed.

4. Place the omelet onto a plate and drizzle the half portion with raspberries. Fold the omelet in half and sprinkle with icing sugar. Using the remaining mixture and ingredients, repeat the same process to create another omelet.

5. Cut the omelet and serve with vanilla ice cream, if desired.

31. Omelette with Black Olives and Mushrooms

Prep Time: 10 minutes
Cook Time: 45 minutes
Ready In: Less than 1 hour
Servings: 6

INGREDIENTS:

10 large eggs
1/2 pound bacon (cooked and chopped into small pieces)
4 dashes hot pepper sauce
1/2 teaspoon salt
1/3 cup milk
1/4 cup green onions (chopped)
3/4 cup Colby-Monterey Jack cheese (shredded)
2 plum tomatoes (chopped)
1 can black olives (drained)
1/3 cup mushrooms (sliced)

DIRECTIONS:

1. Preheat the oven (350 degrees). Get an 8-inch baking dish and spray some cooking spray.

2. Combine milk and eggs in a huge bowl. Beat using an electric mixer until frothy. Sprinkle some salt and add some dashes of hot sauce pepper. Add olives, bacon, green onions, tomatoes, cheese, and mushrooms. Pour into the pan and cover with aluminum foil.

3. Place inside the oven and bake for about 50 minutes until the eggs are set.

4. Remove from the oven and slice according to desired sizes.

CPSIA information can be obtained
at www.ICGtesting.com
Printed in the USA
LVHW03s0519060918
587980LV00004BA/400/P